BRAIN
TRAINING
PUZZLES

— INTERMEDIATE BOOK 1 —

This is a Carlton Book

Published by Carlton Books Limited
20 Mortimer Street
London W1T 3JW

Copyright © 2008 Carlton Books Limited

ISBN 978-1-84732-151-0

Printed in China

BRAIN
TRAINING
PUZZLES

— INTERMEDIATE BOOK 1 —

Introduction

Welcome to brain-training. You are probably here because you don't want to lose any more grey cells, or because you think your brain is getting old, or because your memory isn't what it used to be, or maybe simply because you like puzzles. The good news, whatever your reason for picking up this book, is that if you solve a lot of puzzles you'll be exercising your brain. As with your body, you need to give your brain some exercise to keep it healthy. But remember – looking after your brain isn't just a case of exercise and keeping the cells topped up with water like your car battery – get enough sleep, keep your stress level low and watch what you eat. Strange advice from a puzzle book indeed, but if you really care about your brain you'll look into all of those things – but don't forget to enjoy yourself!

And that brings us back to the puzzles in this book. There are many different types and you can solve them in any order you choose. The best way is to tackle a few puzzles a day and work your way through steadily. If you get stuck, just move on and try a different one; you'll probably find that the one that had you fretting for hours will be easy when you come back to it.

Don't give up, have fun, and above all enjoy!

Piece Puzzle

Only one of these pieces fits the hole in our main picture – the others have all been altered slightly by our artist. Can you place the missing pic?

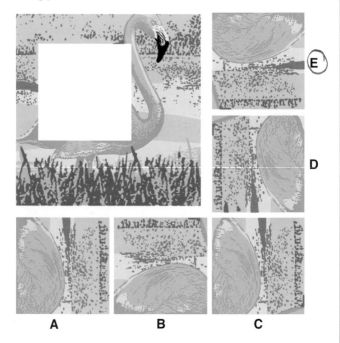

A

B

C

D

E

Answer on page 157

Boxes

Playing the game of boxes, each player takes it in turns to join two adjacent dots with a line. If a player's line completes a box, the player wins the box and has another go. It's your turn in the game below. To avoid giving your opponent a lot of boxes, what's your best move?

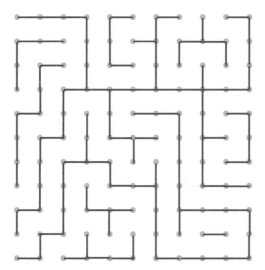

Answer on page 157

Cut and Fold

Which of the patterns below is created by this fold and cut?

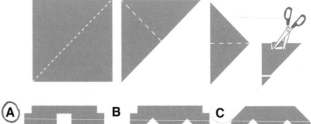

(A)   B   C

Answer on page 157

Dice Maze

On these dice each colour represents a direction – up, down, left and right. Starting in the middle die of the grid, follow the instructions correctly and you will visit every die in turn once only. What's the last die you visit on your trip?

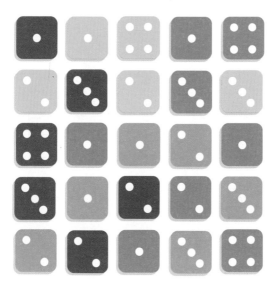

Answer on page 157

Follow That

The sequence below follows a logical pattern. Can you work out the number and colour next in line?

1 2 1 2 1 1 1 ?

Answer on page 157

Magic Squares

Complete the square using nine consecutive numbers, so that all rows, columns and large diagonals add up to the same total.

33

Answer on page 157

Masyu

Draw a single unbroken line around the grid that passes through all the circles. The line must enter and leave each box in the centre of one of its four sides.

Black Circle: Turn left or right in the box, and the line must pass straight through the next and previous boxes.

White Circle: Travel straight through the box, and the line must turn in the next and/or previous box.

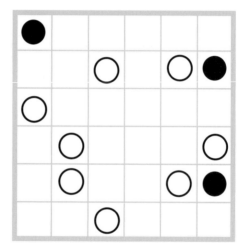

Answer on page 157

Matrix

Which of the four boxed figures completes the set?

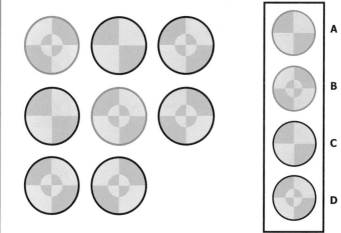

Answer on page 157

Matrix

Which of the boxed figures completes the set?

Answer on page 158

Odd One Out

Which of the shapes below is not the same as the other ones?

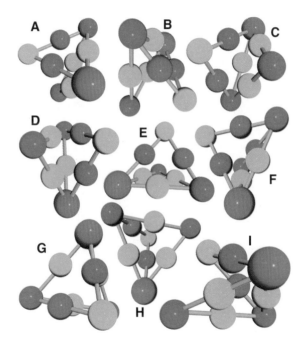

Answer on page 158

Riddle

Kitty has fallen down a well 12 metres deep. He can jump
3 metres up. But slides back 2 metres every time he lands.
How many jumps gets kitty out of the well?

Answer on page 158

Scene It?

The four squares below can all be found in the picture grid – can you track them down? Beware, they may not be the right way up!

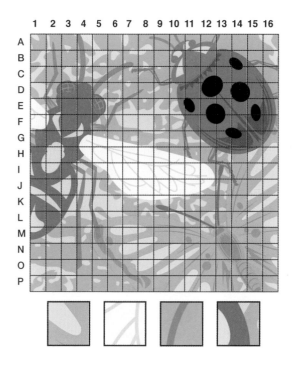

Answer on page 158

Think of a number

At the Sea View Guest house in Bournemouth, England over the course of one week they served 351 glasses of fruit juice with breakfast. 203 of them were orange, 31 were grapefruit, 39 were mango and 78 were apple. Can you work out what proportion of guests had citrus or non-citrus juices?

Answer on page 158

Weigh to Go

The coloured balls represent the numbers 1, 2, 3, 4 and 5. Can you work out which is which, and therefore how many yellow balls are required to balance the final scale?

Answer on page 158

Sudoku

Complete the grid so that all rows and columns, and each outlined block of nine squares, contain the numbers 1, 2, 3, 4, 5, 6, 7, 8 and 9.

		2		1		4		
	5	1		9		7	3	8
7				6		2		
					1		4	5
3				8		9		1
1		4	7					
				4		8		7
4		6	8		2	1	9	
	3					5		

Answer on page 158

Sum People

Work out what number is represented by which person and fill in the
question mark.

11

13

?

14

12   12   19   11

Answer on page 158

Tents and Trees

Every tree 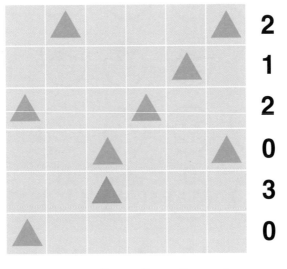 has one tent ▲ found horizontally or vertically adjacent to it. No tent can be in an adjacent square to another tent (even diagonally!). The numbers by each row and column tell you how many tents are there. Can you locate all the tents?

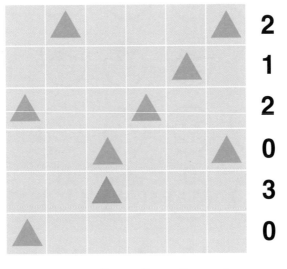

Answer on page 159

Signpost

Can you crack the logical secret behind the distances to these great cities, and work out how far it is to Washington?

BERLIN 16

CARDIFF 20

WASHINGTON ?

AUCKLAND 15

BEIJING 12

Answer on page 159

View from Above

Of the plan views below, only one of them is a true overhead representation of the scene shown here – can you work out which?

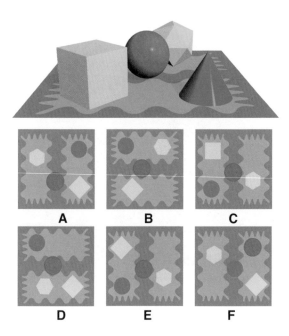

A

B

C

D

E

F

Answer on page 159

Block Party

Assuming all blocks that are not visible from this angle are present, how many blocks have been removed from this 6 x 6 x 6 cube?

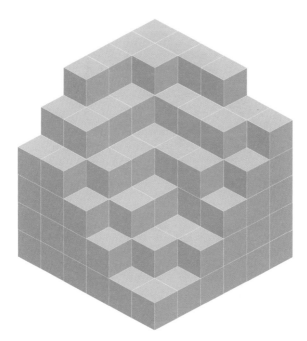

Answer on page 159

Where's the Pair

Only two of the shapes below are exactly the same – can you find the matching pair?

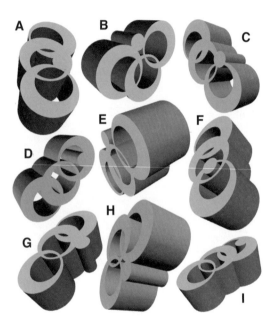

Answer on page 159

Colour Maze

Find the path from one white square to the other. You may only pass from a blue square to a red one, a red to a yellow, a yellow to a purple or a purple to a blue, and you may not travel diagonally.

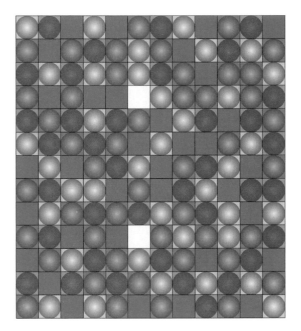

Answer on page 159

Cube Route

Can you crack the colour code and make your way from one yellow square to the other? The blue arrow tells you which way is up...

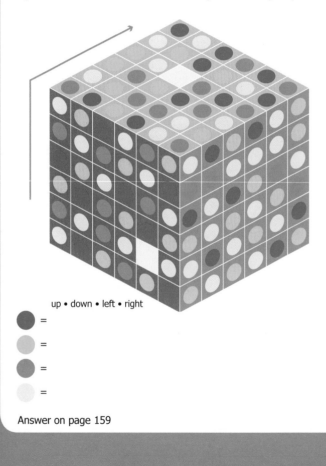

up • down • left • right

○ =

○ =

○ =

○ =

Answer on page 159

Double Drat

All these shapes appear twice in the box except one. Can you spot the singleton?

Answer on page 159

Get the picture

These two grids, when merged together, will make a picture...
Of what?

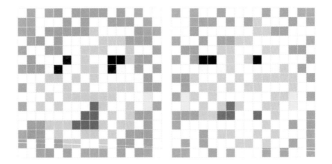

Answer on page 160

Hue Goes There

Three of the sections below can be found in our main grid, one cannot. Can you spot the section that doesn't belong? Beware, the sections might not be the same way round!

A

B

C

D

Answer on page 160

Matrix

Which of the boxed figures completes the set?

Answer on page 160

Mini Nonogram

The numbers by each row and column describe black squares and groups of black squares that are adjoining. Colour in all the black squares and a six number combination will be revealed.

Column clues (top):

	1													
1	1													
1	1				5						1			
1	1				1				3	1				
3	1	5		3	1				1	1	5			
1	1	5		1	1	5		3	1	5				

Row clues (left):

| 3 1 3 |
| 1 1 1 1 |
| 3 1 3 |
| 1 1 1 |
| 3 1 3 |
| |
| 3 3 1 1 |
| 1 1 1 1 1 1 |
| 3 3 3 |
| 1 1 1 |
| 3 3 1 |

Answer on page 160

More or Less

The arrows indicate whether a number in a box is greater or smaller than an adjacent number. Complete the grid so that all rows and columns contain the numbers 1 to 5.

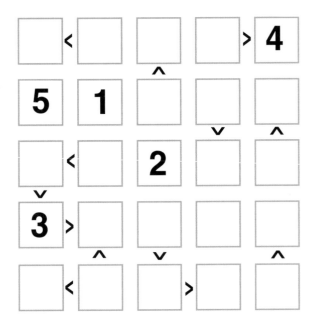

Answer on page 160

Patch of the Day

Place the shape over the grid so that no colour appears twice in the same row or column. Beware, the shape may not be the right way up!

Answer on page 160

Percentage Point

What percentage of this grid is blue and what percentage is yellow?

Answer on page 160

Riddle

Lucy met a pig and a goat in the woods and asked them what day it was, knowing full well that pigs always tell lies on Mondays, Tuesdays and Wednesdays, and that goats always tell lies on Thursdays, Fridays and Saturdays. She asked the pig first. 'Well, yesterday was one of my lying days', he said. She asked the goat. 'Yesterday was one of my lying days too', he said... So what day is it?

Answer on page 160

Scene It?

The four squares below can all be found in the picture grid – can you track them down? Beware, they may not be the right way up!

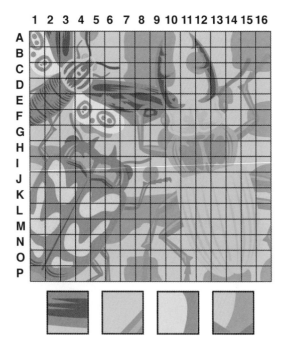

Answer on page 161

Symmetry

This picture, when finished, is symmetrical along a vertical line up the middle. Can you colour in the missing squares and work out what the picture is of?

Answer on page 161

View from Above

Of the plan views below, only one of them is a true overhead representation of the scene shown here – can you work out which?

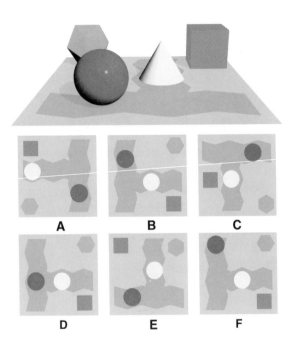

A

B

C

D

E

F

Answer on page 161

Box It

The value of each shape is the number of sides each shape has, multiplied by the number within it. Thus a square containing the number 4 has a value of 16. Find a block two squares wide and two squares high with a total value of exactly 50.

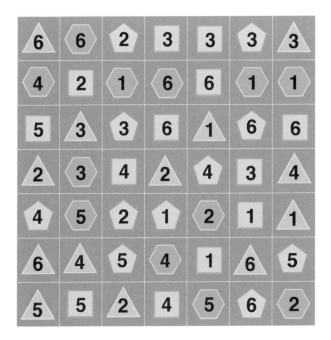

Answer on page 161

Boxes

Playing the game of boxes, each player takes it in turns to join two adjacent dots with a line. If a player's line completes a box, the player wins the box and has another go. It's your turn in the game below. To avoid giving your opponent a lot of boxes, what's your best move?

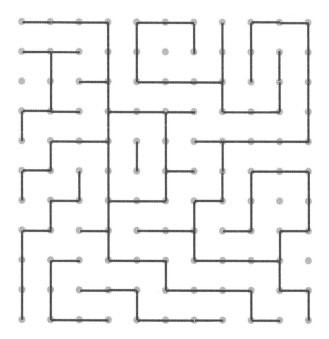

Answer on page 161

Tree Tent

Every tree ▲ has one tent ▲ found horizontally or vertically adjacent to it. No tent can be in an adjacent square to another tent (even diagonally). The numbers by each row and column tell you how many tents are there. Can you locate all the tents?

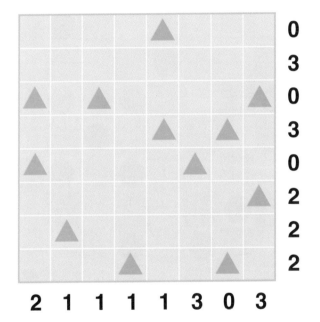

Answer on page 161

Checkers

Make a move for white so that eight black pieces are left, none of which are in the same column or row.

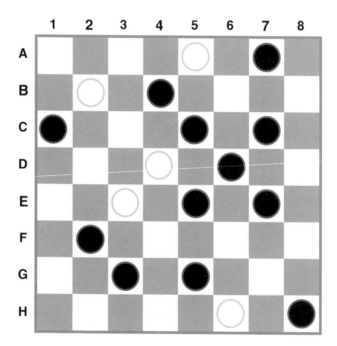

Answer on page 161

Dice Puzzle

What's the missing number?

15   12   16   ?

Answer on page 161

Figure it Out

The sequence 23224 can be found once in the grid, reading up, down, backwards, forwards or diagonally. Can you pick it out?

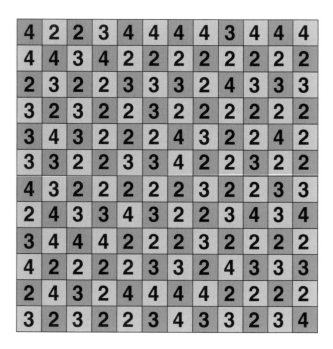

4	2	2	3	4	4	4	4	3	4	4	4
4	4	3	4	2	2	2	2	2	2	2	2
2	3	2	2	3	3	3	2	4	3	3	3
3	2	3	2	2	3	2	2	2	2	2	2
3	4	3	2	2	2	4	3	2	2	4	2
3	3	2	2	3	3	4	2	2	3	2	2
4	3	2	2	2	2	2	3	2	2	3	3
2	4	3	3	4	3	2	2	3	4	3	4
3	4	4	4	2	2	2	3	2	2	2	2
4	2	2	2	2	3	3	2	4	3	3	3
2	4	3	2	4	4	4	4	2	2	2	2
3	2	3	2	2	3	4	3	3	2	3	4

Answer on page 162

Game of Three Halves

Which three shapes below will piece together to create the top shape?

A

B

C

D

E

F

Answer on page 162

Gridlock

Which square correctly completes the grid?

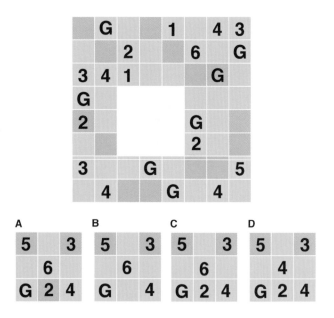

A

5		3
	6	
G	2	4

B

5		3
	6	
G		4

C

5		3
	6	
G	2	4

D

5		3
	4	
G	2	4

Answer on page 162

Latin Square

Complete the grid so that every row and column, and every outlined area, contains the letters A, B, C, D, E and F.

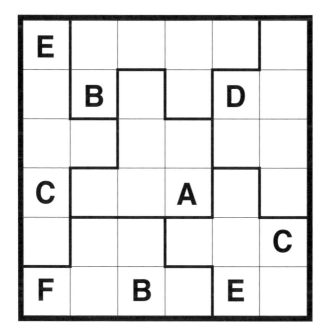

Answer on page 162

Looplink

Connect adjacent dots with either horizontal or vertical lines to create a continuous unbroken loop which never crosses over itself. Some, but not all of the boxes are numbered. The numbers in these boxes tell you how many sides of that box are used by your unbroken line.

Answer on page 162

Masyu

Draw a single unbroken line around the grid that passes through all the circles. The line must enter and leave each box in the centre of one of its four sides. Black Circle: Turn left or right in the box, and the line must pass straight through the next and previous boxes. White Circle: Travel straight through the box, and the line must turn in the next and/or previous box.

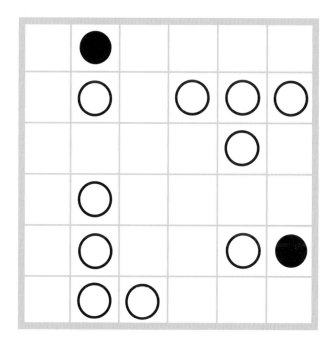

Answer on page 162

Matrix

Which of the boxed figures completes the set?

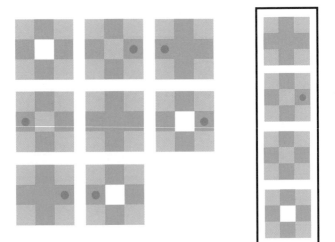

Answer on page 162

Mirror Image

Only one of these pictures is an exact mirror image of the first one. Can you spot it?

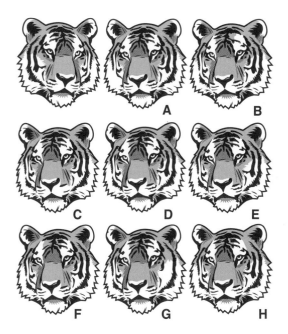

Answer on page 162

More or Less

The arrows indicate whether a number in a box is greater or smaller than an adjacent number. Complete the grid so that all rows and columns contain the numbers 1 to 6.

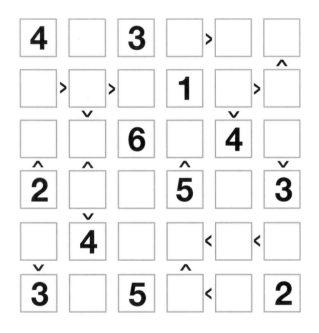

Answer on page 163

Odd One Out

Which of the shapes below is not the same as the other ones?

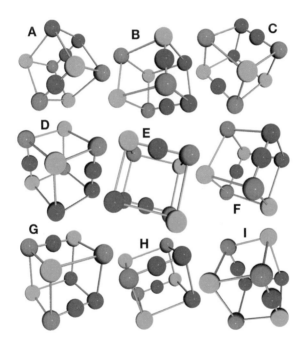

Answer on page 163

Picture Parts

Which box has exactly the right bits to make the pic?

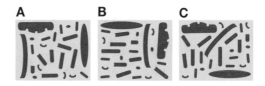

A   **B**   **C**

Answer on page 163

Pots of Dots

How many dots should there be in the hole in this pattern?

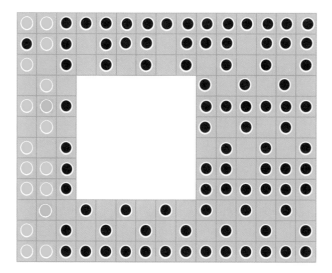

Answer on page 163

Riddle

Little Joe was saving up for a scarf to wear to the big football match. On the first day of he month, he saved one penny, on the second, 2, on the third, 3 and so on until on the day of the match he had exactly the three pounds required to buy the scarf. What day was the game?

Answer on page 163

Safecracker

To open the safe, all the buttons must be pressed in the correct order before the "open" button is pressed. What is the first button pressed in your sequence?

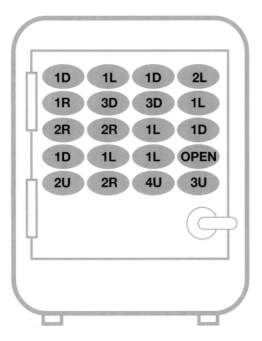

Answer on page 163

Scales

Can you arranged the supplied weights in such a way as to balance the whole scale?

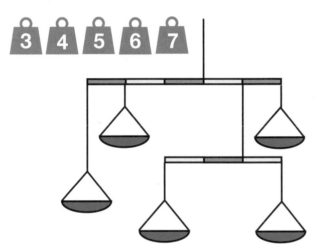

Answer on page 163

Shape Shifting

Fill in the empty squares so that each row, column and long diagonal contains five different coloured balls.

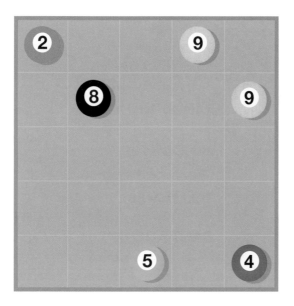

Answer on page 163

Signpost

Can you crack the logical secret behind the distances to these great cities, and work out how far it is to Vancouver?

GENEVA 34

EDINBURGH 17

VANCOUVER ?

TALLINN 86

SANTIAGO 80

Answer on page 164

Spot the Difference

Can you spot ten differences between this pair of pictures?

Answer on page 164

Sudoku Sixpack

Complete the grid so that every row, column and long diagonal contains the numbers 1, 2, 3, 4, 5 and 6.

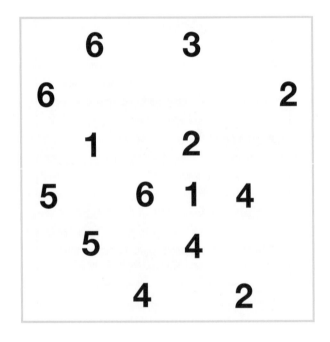

Answer on page 164

Sum People

Work out what number is represented by which person and fill in the question mark.

28
18
27
10

26 16 ? 21

Answer on page 164

Think of a Number

Officers Kaplutski and Wojowitz were counting up how many jaywalkers they had arrested in a week. Kaplutski was happy to discover he was ahead 14 to 11. Can you express the two cops success rate as a percentage?

Answer on page 164

Venn Diagrams

Can you work out which areas of this diagram represent Australian teetotal surfers who don't play rugby, and non-Australian beer drinking rugby players that don't surf?

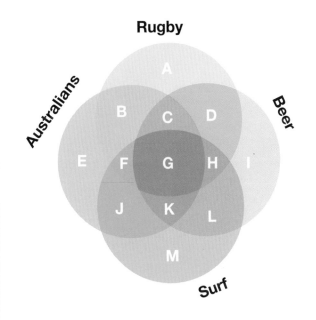

Answer on page 164

Weigh to Go

The coloured balls represent the numbers 1, 2, 3, 4 and 5. Can you work out which is which, and therefore how many purple balls are required to balance the final scale?

Answer on page 164

Matrix

Which of the boxed figures completes the set?

Answer on page 164

Where's the Pair?

Only two of the shapes below are exactly the same – can you find the matching pair?

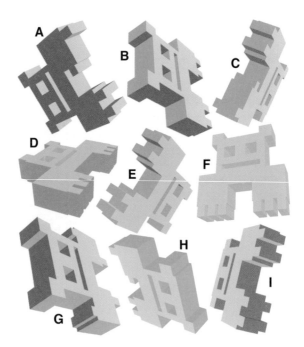

Answer on page 165

All Change

The colour of each triangle in pattern B is directly related to the colours in pattern A. Can you apply the same rules and fill in pattern C?

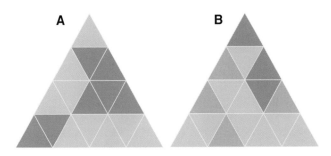

A

B

C

Answer on page 165

Bits and Pieces

These ten pieces can be asembled to spell the name of a movie star... Who?

Answer on page 165

Cube Route

Can you crack the colour code and make your way from one orange square to the other? The blue arrow tells you which way is up...

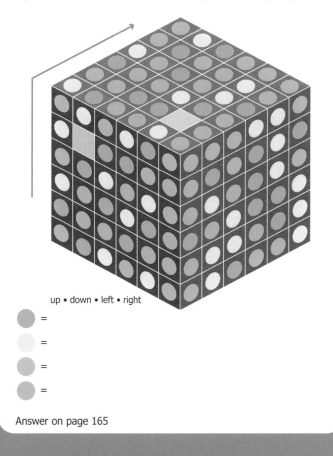

up • left • down • right

● =

○ =

● =

● =

Answer on page 165

Finding Nemo

The word NEMO can be found once in the grid, reading up, down, backwards, forwards or diagonally. Can you pick it out?

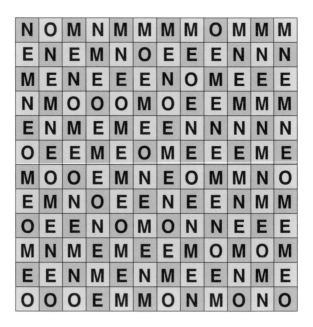

N	O	M	N	M	M	M	M	O	M	M
E	N	E	M	N	O	E	E	E	N	N
M	E	N	E	E	E	N	O	M	E	E
N	M	O	O	O	M	O	E	E	M	M
E	N	M	E	M	E	E	N	N	N	N
O	E	E	M	E	O	M	E	E	E	M	E
M	O	O	E	M	N	E	O	M	M	N	O
E	M	N	O	E	E	N	E	E	N	M	M
O	E	E	N	O	M	O	N	N	E	E	E
M	N	M	E	M	E	E	M	O	M	O	M
E	E	N	M	E	N	M	E	E	N	M	E
O	O	O	E	M	M	O	N	M	O	N	O

Answer on page 165

Hue Goes There

Three of the sections below can be found in our main grid, one cannot. Can you spot the section that doesn't belong? Beware, the sections might not be the same way round!

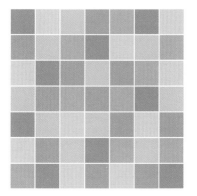

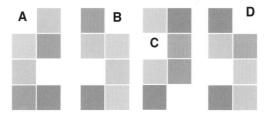

Answer on page 165

Magic Squares

Complete the square using nine consecutive numbers, so that all rows, columns and large diagonals add up to the same total.

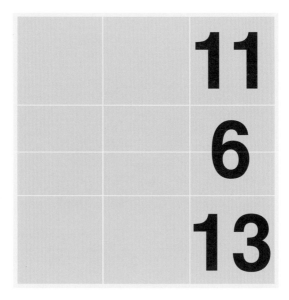

Answer on page 165

Matrix

Which of the boxed figures completes the set?

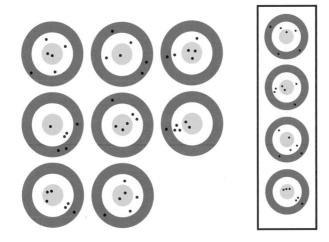

Answer on page 165

Odd Clocks

Auckland is 16 hours ahead of Sao Paulo, which is 1 hour ahead of Miami. It is 2.15 pm on Saturday in Sao Paulo – what time is it in the other two cities?

SAO PAULO

MIAMI   **AUCKLAND**

Answer on page 166

Riddle

Jessica promised Julia that she would tell her a huge piece of gossip, but it would have to wait until the day before four days from the day after tomorrow. Today is Wednesday the 3rd – when does Julia get to know?

Answer on page 166

Safecracker

To open the safe, all the buttons must be pressed in the correct order before the "open" button is pressed. What is the first button pressed in your sequence?

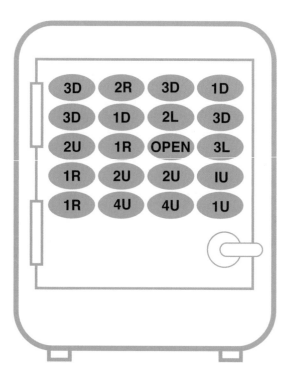

3D	2R	3D	1D
3D	1D	2L	3D
2U	1R	OPEN	3L
1R	2U	2U	IU
1R	4U	4U	1U

Answer on page 166

Logic Sequence

The balls below have been rearranged. Can you work out the new sequence of the balls from the clues given below?

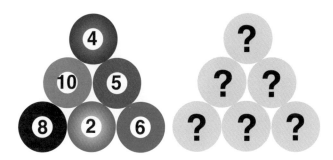

The 4 ball isn't touching the 5 or the 2.
The 8 ball is touching four others.
The 4 ball is immediately to the right of the 6.
The 10 ball is resting on two balls totalling 13.

Answer on page 166

Knight's Move

Find an empty square in the grid that is one chess knight's move away from a blue, red and yellow circle. A knight's move is an 'L' shape – two squares sideways, up or down in any direction, followed by one square to the left or right.

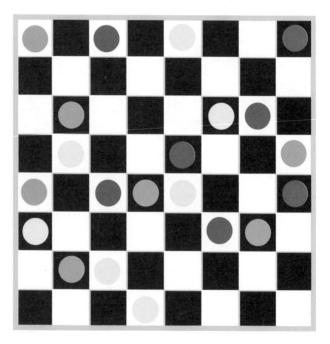

Answer on page 166

Boxes

Playing the game of boxes, each player takes it in turns to join two adjacent dots with a line. If a player's line completes a box, the player wins the box and has another go. It's your turn in the game below. To avoid giving your opponent a lot of boxes, what's your best move?

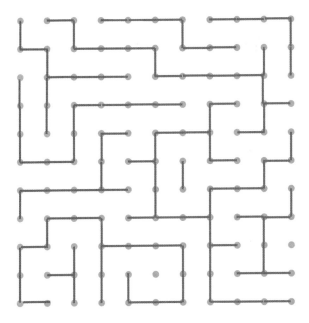

Answer on page 166

X and O

The numbers around the edge of the grid describe the number of X's in the vertical, horizontal and diagonal lines connecting with that square. Complete the grid so that there is an X or O in every square.

2	4	5	4	2	7	1
5	X			X		4
4						3
3						6
2			O			4
5	O			X		5
1	2	4	3	4	6	2

Answer on page 166

Think Back

Study these images for a minute, then cover them and answer the five questions below.

Questions:
1. How many of the yellow stars are on blue circles?
2. How many red circles are there?
3. Counting stars, circles and backgrounds, how many are blue in total?
4. What colour background has the red circle?
5. What colour star has the yellow background?

Answer on page 166

Sudoku

Fill in each row, column and 9x9 box with the numbers 1, 2, 3, 4, 5, 6, 7, 8, 9 once only.

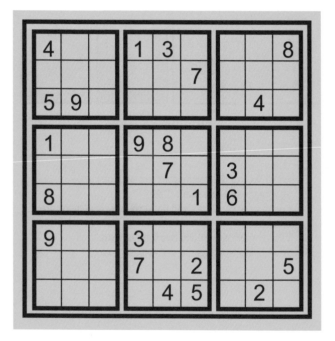

Answer on page 167

Spot the Difference

Can you spot ten differences between this pair of pictures?

Answer on page 167

Same Difference

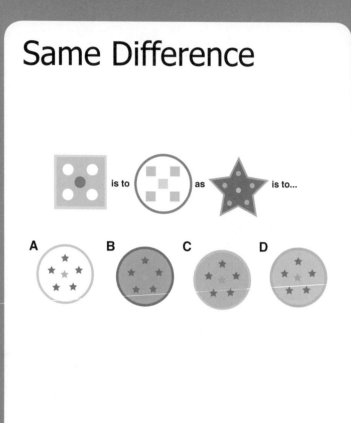

is to

as

is to...

A   B   C   D

Answer on page 167

Percentage Point

What percentage of this shape is blue and what percentage is orange?

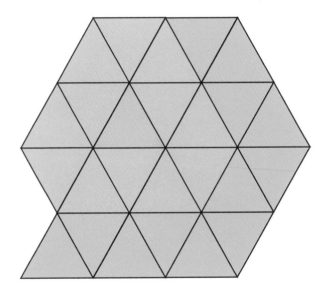

Answer on page 167

Pots of Dots

How many dots should there be in the hole in this pattern?

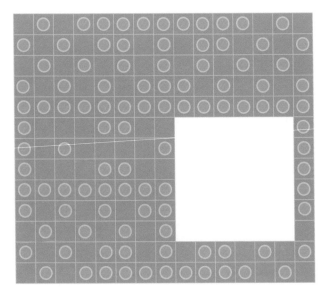

Answer on page 167

Checkers

Make a move for white so that eight black pieces are left, none of which are in the same column or row.

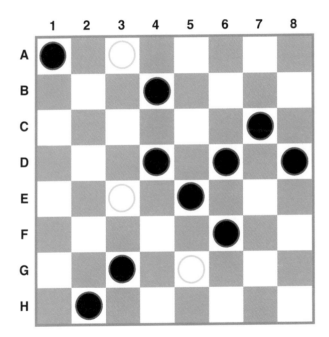

Answer on page 167

Follow That

The sequence below follows a logical pattern. Can you work out what colour face follows, and if it should be smiling?

 **?**

Answer on page 167

Latin Square

Complete the grid so that every row and column, and every outlined area, contains the letters A, B, C, D, E and F.

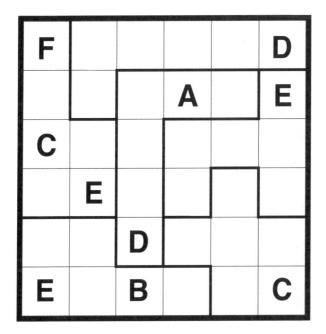

Answer on page 167

Location

Below is an altered view of a world-famous landmark. Can you tell where it is?

Answer on page 168

Matrix

Which of the boxed figures completes the set?

Answer on page 168

Piece Puzzle

Only one of these pieces fits the hole in our main picture – the others have all been altered slightly by our artist. Can you place the missing pic?

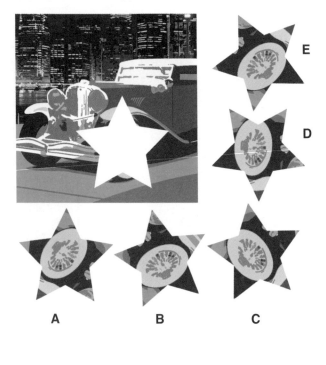

E

D

A

B

C

Answer on page 168

Pool Puzzle

You're playing stripes in a game of pool, and you've cleaned up all your balls. You're snookered on the black though... Can you spot the shot?

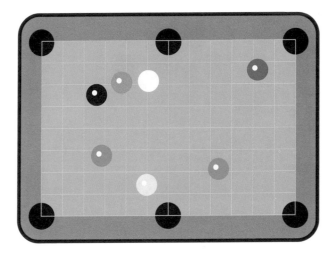

Answer on page 168

Number Mountain

Replace the question marks with numbers so that each pair of blocks adds up to the block directly above them.

Answer on page 168

Picture Parts

Which box has exactly the right bits to make the pic?

A   B   C

Answer on page 168

Riddle

Belinda, Benny, Bobby, Brian and Bill entered a competition to guess how many sweets there were in a jar. Belinda said 300, Ben said 280, Bobby said 290, Brian said 250 and Bill said 260. Two guesses were just ten sweets away from the number. One guess was 40 away and another was wrong by 30. But who won?

Answer on page 168

Sudoku

Complete the grid so that all rows and columns, and each outlined block of nine squares, contain the numbers 1, 2, 3, 4, 5, 6, 7, 8 and 9.

	6	2			8	5		7
1				3		9		
	8			9			2	
	7			8		3	4	
		1		5				
5						8	1	6
2	1		6	5		7		
		3						
8				2	3		9	1

Answer on page 168

Sum People

Work out what number is represented by which person and fill in the question mark.

Answer on page 169

Think of a Number

Old Mother Jones loves her gummy sweets. They come in three colours: orange, red and yellow. There were exactly twice as many red sweets as yellow ones in the packet. After eating seven orange ones, she had one less orange than yellow left, and the number of orange sweets remaining represented 20 percent of the sweets she started with. How many did she start with?

Answer on page 169

Weigh to Go

The coloured balls represent the numbers 1, 2, 3, 4 and 5. Can you work out which is which, and therefore how many red balls are required to balance the final scale?

Answer on page 169

Rainbow Reckoning

The crazy paving around this fountain will use just Gold, Black and Cream stones. No two stones that touch each other can be the same colour. What colour will the stone under the proposed sundial?

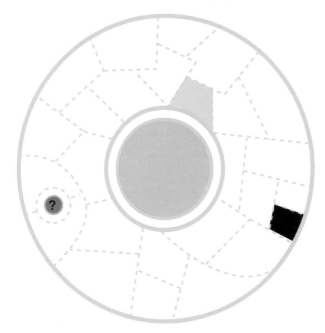

Answer on page 169

Shuffle

Fill up the shuffle box so that each row, column and long diagonal contains a Jack, Queen, King and Ace of each suit.

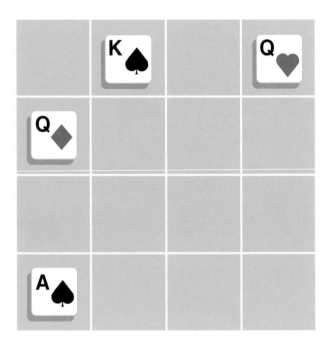

Answer on page 169

Mini Nonogram

The numbers by each row and column describe black squares and groups of black squares that are adjoining. Colour in all the black squares and a six number combination will be revealed.

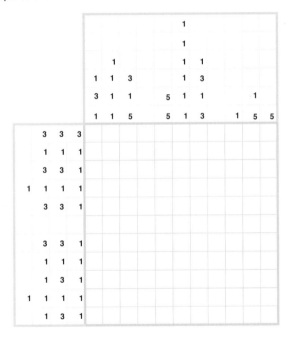

Answer on page 169

Double Drat

All these shapes appear twice in the box except one. Can you spot the singleton?

Answer on page 169

Where's the Pair?

Only two of these pictures are exactly the same. Can you spot the matching pair?

Answer on page 169

The Red Corner

Use the red corners to make the central number the same way in all three cases. What number should replace the question mark?

Answer on page 170

Hub Signs

What numbers should appear in the hubs of these number wheels?

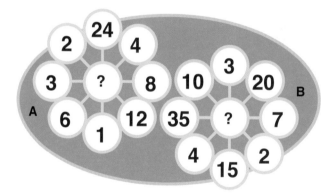

Answer on page 170

Box It

The value of each shape is the number of sides each shape has, multiplied by the number within it. Thus a square containing the number 4 has a value of 16. Find a block two squares wide and two squares high with a total value of exactly 100.

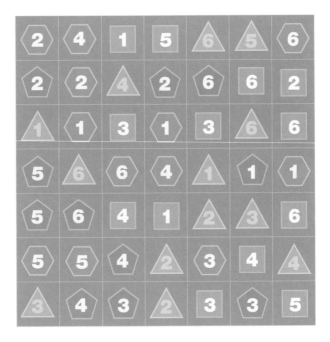

Answer on page 170

Revolutions

Cog A has 10 teeth, cog B has 8 and cog C has 14. How many revolutions must cog A turn through to bring all three cogs back to these exact positions?

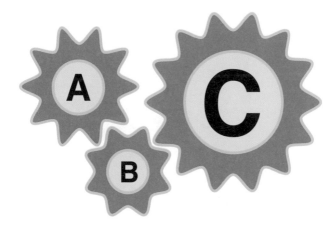

Answer on page 170

Riddle

Ada the antique dealer was pondering her profits one day, and thinking how she could improve them. She looked at the Victorian clock she was selling for a 5% profit, and worked out that had she bought it for 10% less and sold it at the same price she would have made a £15 profit. How much did she buy it for?

Answer on page 170

All Change

The colour of each square in pattern B is directly related to the colours in pattern A. The square colours in pattern C relate to pattern B the same way. Can you apply the same the rules and fill in pattern D?

A

B

C

D

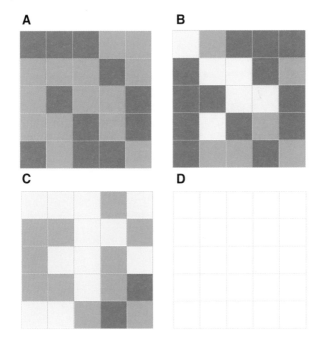

Answer on page 170

Where's the Pair?

Only two of the shapes below are exactly the same, can you find the matching pair?

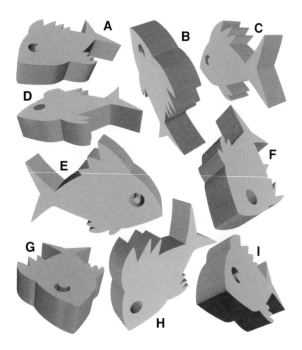

Answer on page 170

All Change

The colour of each hexagon in pattern B is directly related to the colours in pattern A. Can you apply the same rules and fill in pattern C?

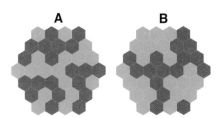

Answer on page 170

Cats and Cogs

Turn the handle in the indicated direction... Does the cat go up or down?

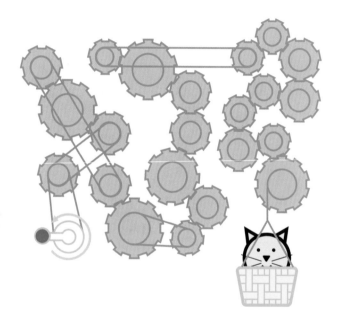

Answer on page 171

Cut and Fold

Which of the patterns below is created by this fold and cut?

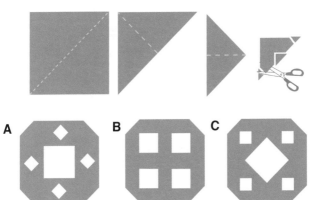

A

B

C

Answer on page 171

Get the Picture

These two grids, when merged together, will make a picture... Of what?

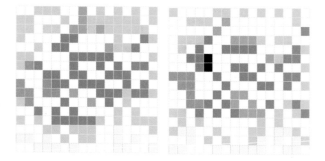

Answer on page 171

More or Less

The arrows indicate whether a number in a box is greater or smaller than an adjacent number. Complete the grid so that all rows and columns contain the numbers 1 to 6.

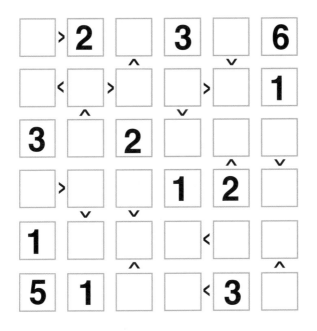

Answer on page 171

Patch of the Day

Place the shape over the grid so that no colour appears twice in the same row or column. Beware, the shape may not be the right way up!

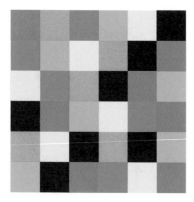

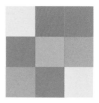

Answer on page 171

Riddle

Mr and Mrs Toggle were driving from Aystown to Beestown on vacation when Mr T accidentally ran down a signpost at a road junction. The post was fine, completely unharmed. But how do they know which way Beestown is now?

Answer on page 171

Scene It?

The four squares below can all be found in the picture grid – can you track them down? Beware, they may not be the right way up!

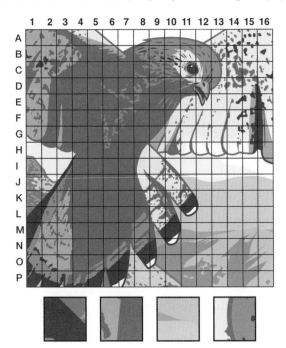

Answer on page 171

Shape Shifting

Fill in the empty squares so that each row, column and long diagonal contains six different symbols

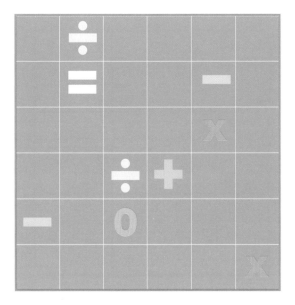

Answer on page 171

Sudoku

Complet the grid so that all rows and columns, and each outlined block of nine squares, contain the numbers 1, 2, 3, 4, 5, 6, 7, 8 and 9.

5	1			2		4	9	8
	3		1		6		7	5
	8				4	6		
	7	3			9		8	
1				7		9		2
	2		3		5	1		
	5		8	6			4	
	9	2					5	6
8		4		9	7	3		

Answer on page 172

Block Party

Assuming all blocks that are not visible from this angle are present,
how many blocks have been removed from this 5 x 5 x 5 cube?

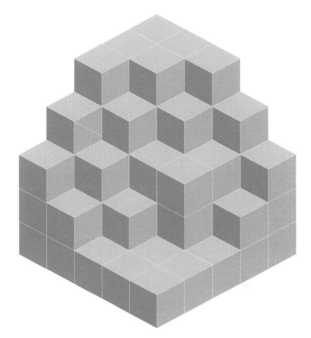

Answer on page 172

Chess

Can you place a queen, a bishop, a knight and a rook on this chessboard board so that the red squares are attacked by exactly two pieces, and the green ones by 3 pieces?

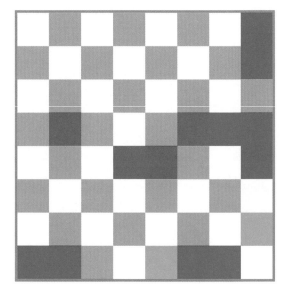

Answer on page 172

Double Maze

Make your way from A to B without passing through any yellow squares — then do it again without passing through any blue squares!

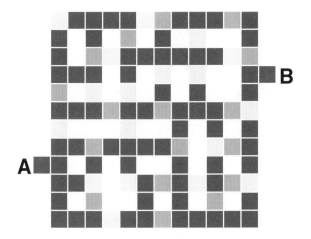

Answer on page 172

Cubism

The shape below can be folded to make a cube. Which of the four cubes picured below could it make?

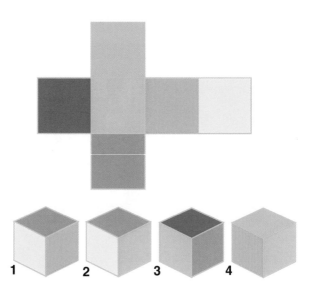

1   2   3   4

Answer on page 172

Odd One Out

Which of the shapes below is not the same as the other ones?

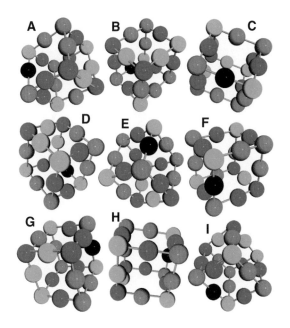

Answer on page 172

Radar

The numbers in some cells in the grid indicate the exact number of black cells that should border it. Shade these black, until all the numbers are surrounded by the correct number of black cells.

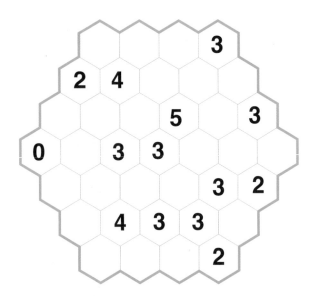

Answer on page 172

Shuffle

Fill up the shuffle box so that each row, column and long diagonal contains a Jack, Queen, King and Ace of each suit.

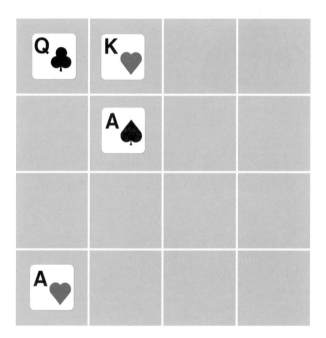

Answer on page 172

Silhouette

Which of the coloured in pics matches our silhouette?

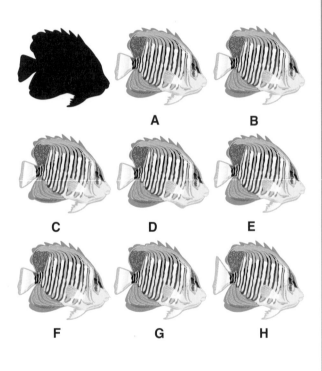

A

B

C

D

E

F

G

H

Answer on page 173

Symbol Sums

These symbols represent the numbers 1 to 4. If the pink parrot represents the number 2, can you work out what the other colour parrots are representing and make a working sum?

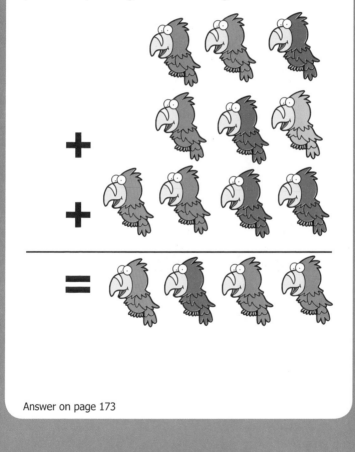

Answer on page 173

Scene It?

The four squares below can all be found in the picture grid – can you track them down? Beware, they may not be the right way up!

Answer on page 173

In the Area

Can you work out the approximate area that this camel is occupying?

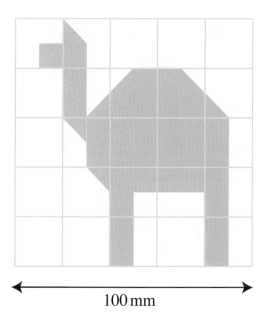

100 mm

Answer on page 173

Sudoku Sixpack

Complete the grid so that every row, column and long diagonal contains the numbers 1, 2, 3, 4, 5 and 6.

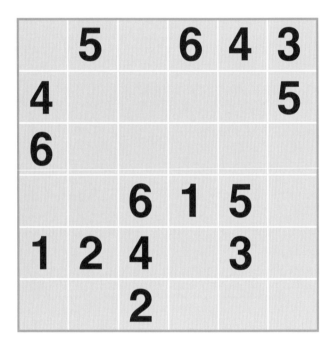

Answer on page 173

Tents and Trees

Every tree 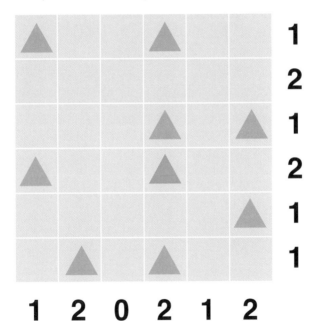 has one tent ▲ found horizontally or vertically adjacent to it. No tent can be in an adjacent square to another tent (even diagonally!). The numbers by each row and column tell you how many tents are there. Can you locate all the tents?

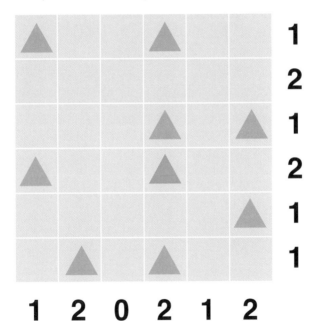

Answer on page 173

Swatch Switch

One of our swatches is missing! Can you work out the four colour sequence that completes the set?

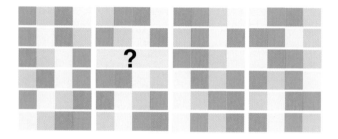

Answer on page 173

Floor Fillers

Below is a plan of the entrance pathway to a theatre, complete with spaces either side for plant pots. Below are some oddly shaped pieces of red carpet... Can you fill the floor with them?

Answer on page 173

Gridlock

Which square correctly completes the grid?

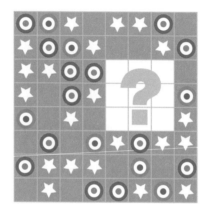

A **B** **C** **D**

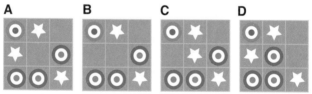

Answer on page 174

Looplink

Connect adjacent dots with either horizontal or vertical lines to create a continuous unbroken loop which never crosses over itself. The numbers in these boxes tell you how many sides of that box are used by your unbroken line.

3	2	2	2	3
3	1	1	2	2
3	0	2	2	2
3	2	3	2	3
3	1	2	2	2

Answer on page 174

Magic Squares

Complete the square using nine consecutive numbers, so that all rows, columns and large diagonals add up to the same total.

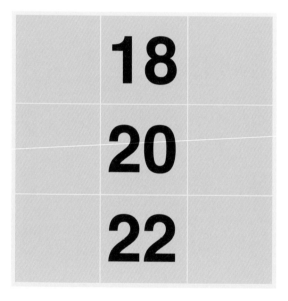

Answer on page 174

Shape Stacker

Can you work out the logic behind the numbers in these shapes, and suggest what number the question mark represents?

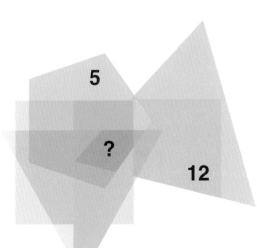

Answer on page 174

Odd Clocks

Rio is 6 hours behind Athens, which is 2 hours behind Karachi.
It is 1.25 am on Thursday in Athens – what time is it in the other
two cities?

ATHENS

KARACHI

RIO

Answer on page 174

Picture Parts

Which box has exactly the right bits to make the pic?

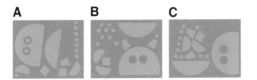

A   B   C

Answer on page 174

Signpost

Can you crack the logical secret behind the distances to these great cities, and work out how far it is to Hong Kong?

NEW YORK 28

GLASGOW 14

HONG KONG ?

BARCELONA 8

COLOMBO 9

Answer on page 175

Matrix

Which of the boxed figures completes the set?

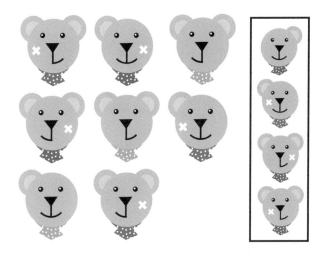

Answer on page 174

Mirror Image

Only one of these pictures is an exact mirror image of the first one?
Can you spot it?

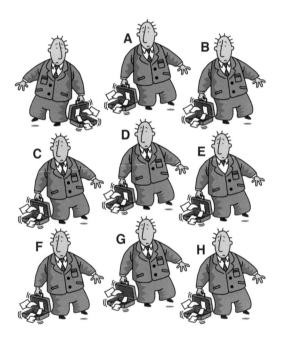

Answer on page 175

Number Sweep

The numbers in some squares in the grid indicate the exact number of black squares that should surround it. Shade these squares until all the numbers are surrounded by the correct number of black squares, and a number will be revealed!

0	2		5		5		5		5		2
	4			8		8		8		5	
2		7	8		6		5		5		2
	5		8			6		6		3	
4		8		7	6		5		4		1
	7		7		5			7		5	
3		5		4		3	5		8		4
	6		4		0		3			8	
3		5		4		3		6	8		5
	7		7		5		6		8		
3		6		8		8		7		4	3
	2		4		5		5		4		1

Answer on page 175

Scales

The arms of these scales are divided into sections – a weight two sections away from the middle will be twice as heavy as a weight one section away. Can you arranged the supplied weights in such a way as to balance the whole scale?

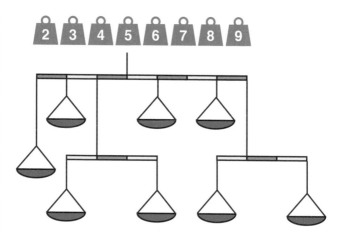

Answer on page 175

Spot the Difference

Can you spot ten differences between this pair of pictures?

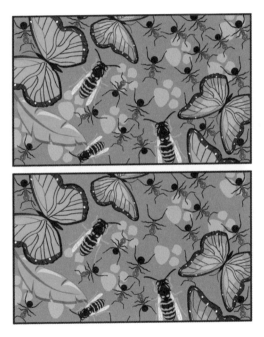

Answer on page 175

Sudoku

Complete the grid so that all rows and columns, and each outlined block of nine squares, contain the numbers 1, 2, 3, 4, 5, 6, 7, 8 and 9.

	1			3	6		2	9
9	2	8			7	3	6	
		7					4	8
	5		3		1	4		6
8		6		2	9	5	1	7
	7	4			8			3
5		3			2		7	
		2	7	8		9	5	1
	9		5		4			

Answer on page 175

Spot the Difference

Can you spot ten differences between this pair of pictures?

Answer on page 175

Answers

Page 6
Answer: E

Page 7

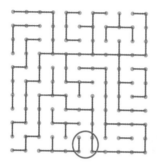

Solution: A line on the top or bottom of this square will only give up one box to your opponent

Page 8
Answer: A

Page 9
Answer:
Blue = Left
Red = Right
Green = Up
Yellow = Down
The final die in your trip is the

Blue 1, three dice down in the second column

Page 10
Answer: A red 2. Two numbers the same are followed by a red number. Two numbers of different colours are followed by a 2

Page 11

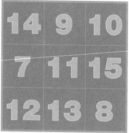

Page 12

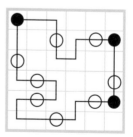

Answers

Page 13

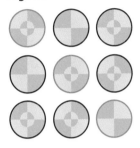

Solution: Each vertical and horizontal line contains one shape with a red outline and two shapes with a black outline. Each line also contains one shape where the inner quartered circle has been removed and one shape that has been rotated through 90 degrees. The missing shape should not be rotated, it should have a red outline and the inner circle should be missing

Page 14

Solution: Each line contains two pyramids with golden balls on top, and one without.
Each line contains two pyramids with a blue 'B', and one without.
Each line contains two pyramids with a hole and one without.
Each line contains one image that has been rotated through 90 degrees.
The missing image should be a pyramid with a golden ball on top, without a blue 'B', but with a hole, and rotated through 90 degrees

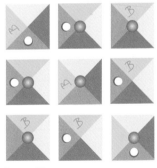

Page 15
Answer: F is the odd one out

Answers

Page 16
Answer: 10. On the 10th jump he makes it!

Page 17
Answer: I15, 19, A9, M1

Page 18
Answer: Two thirds and one third. 351 divided by 3 is 117 (39 + 78) 117 × 2 = 234 (203 + 31)

Page 19
Answer: Purple = 1, Green = 2, Red = 3, Yellow = 4, Blue = 5. Four Yellow balls are required

Page 20

9	8	2	3	1	7	4	5	6
6	5	1	2	9	4	7	3	8
7	4	3	5	6	8	2	1	9
8	6	7	9	2	1	3	4	5
3	2	5	4	8	6	9	7	1
1	9	4	7	3	5	6	8	2
5	1	9	6	4	3	8	2	7
4	7	6	8	5	2	1	9	3
2	3	8	1	7	9	5	6	4

Page 21
Solution: 16

 2

 3

4

 5

Page 22

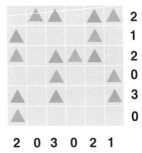

2
1
2
0
3
0

2 0 3 0 2 1

Answers

Page 23
Answer: 42
Score one for a consonant
and two for a vowel, then
multiply the totals together.
$6 \times 7 = 42$

Page 24
Answer: E

Page 25
Answer: 68

Page 26
Answer: B and H are the pair

Page 27

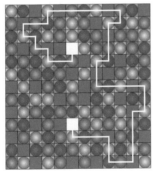

Page 28

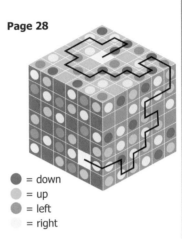

● = down
○ = up
● = left
○ = right

Page 29

Page 30

Answers

Page 31
Answer: C is the odd shape out

Page 32
Solution: Each vertical and horizontal line contains one shape with a small yellow inner square, one with a small white inner square, and one with a small orange inner square. Each vertical and horizontal line also contains one shape with a larger yellow square, one with a larger white square, and one with a larger orange square. The missing shape must contain a small yellow inner square and a larger yellow square. Of course orange squares are invisible against an orange background

Page 33
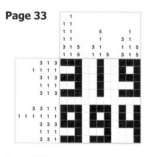

Page 34

Page 35

Page 36
44% is blue, 56% is yellow. 11 out of 25 squares in the grid are blue, 14 are yellow. Multiply both numbers by 4 and you see a percentage

Page 37
Answer: Thursday. The goat is lying!

Answers

Page 38
Answer: D6, O10, N3, I1

Page 39

Page 40
Answer: B

Page 41

Page 42

Solution: A line on the left or bottom of this square will only give up one box to your opponent

Page 43

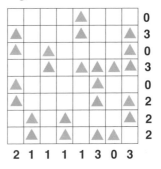

Page 44

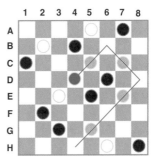

Page 45
Answer: 4. Subtract the right face from the front face and multiply by the top one

Answers

Page 46

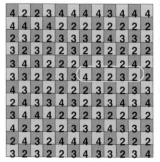

Page 47
Solution:
A, B, and D

Page 48
Answer: C. Each row and column in the grid contains two green squares and a letter G, and numbers that total 8

Page 49

E	C	A	D	F	B
A	B	C	E	D	F
D	F	E	B	C	A
C	D	F	A	B	E
B	E	D	F	A	C
F	A	B	C	E	D

Page 50

Page 51

Page 52
Solution: Each vertical and

 horizontal line contains one shape with a central green square, one with a central white square, and one with a central pink square.

Each vertical and horizontal line also contains one shape with a blue dot on the left, one with a blue dot on the right, and one with no blue dot. The missing shape should have a central green square and no blue dot

162

Answers

Page 53
Answer: E

Page 54

Page 55
Answer: B is the odd one out

Page 56
Answer: A

Page 57
Solution: 25

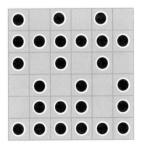

Page 58
Answer: The game was on the 24th day of the month

Page 59

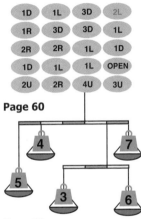

Page 60

Page 61

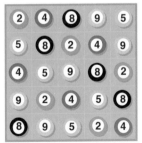

Answers

Page 62
Answer: 92
Multiply the alphabetical position of the first letter of each city by 5, then subtract the alphabetical position of the last letter 22 x 5 = 110 − 18 = 92

Page 63

Page 64

2	6	5	3	1	4
6	4	1	5	3	2
4	1	3	2	5	6
5	2	6	1	4	3
3	5	2	4	6	1
1	3	4	6	2	5

Page 65
Solution: 20

😊 1

👩 3

😊 7

😄 12

Page 66
Answer: Kaplutski 56 percent, Wojowitz 44 percent. The total number is 25. Multiply this number, and the others, by 4 to get percentages

Page 67
Answer: J and D

Page 68
Solution: Red = 1, Purple = 2, Green = 3, Blue = 4, Yellow = 5. Five purple balls are required.

Page 69
Answer: Each vertical and horizontal line contains one shape with two stars, one with three, and one with four. Each line also contains one shape a blue moon, one with a pink moon and one with a white moon. Each line also contains one orange sky and two blue ones, and each line contains one moon pointing right and two pointing left. The missing shape should contain

 four stars and a blue sky, and the moon should be white and facing right.

Answers

Page 70
Answer: C and H are the pair

Page 71
Solution: If its bordering triangles are predominantly green, a triangle becomes green. If they are predominantly purple, it becomes purple. If the bordering cells are equal in number, the triangle becomes pink, and if the bordering triangles have now become predominantly pink, it also becomes pink

Page 72
Answer: Tom Cruise

Page 73

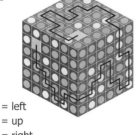

● = left
○ = up
● = right
● = down

Page 74

Page 75
Answer: C is the odd shape out

Page 76

7	12	11
14	10	6
9	8	13

Page 77

Solution: Each line contains one target with three holes in the gold, two holes in the white and one hole in the red.
Each line contains one target with three holes in the white, two holes in the gold and one hole in the red.
Each line contains one target with three holes in the red, two holes in the white and one hole in the gold.
The missing picture must have three holes in the red, two holes in the white and one in the gold

Answers

Page 78
Answer:
3.15 pm on Saturday in Miami
6.15 am on Sunday in Auckland

Page 79
Answer: Monday the 8th

Page 80

Page 81

Page 82

Page 83
Solution: A line on the left or right of this square will only give up one box to your opponent

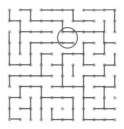

Page 84

2	4	5	4	2	7	1
5	X	X	O	X	O	4
4	O	O	X	O	X	3
3	O	X	O	O	X	6
2	O	X	O	O	X	4
5	O	O	O	X	X	5
1	2	4	3	4	6	2

Page 85
Answers:
1. None
2. 1
3. 3
4. Blue
5. Red

Answers

Page 86

4	7	2	1	3	9	5	6	8
3	8	6	4	5	7	2	1	9
5	9	1	2	6	8	7	4	3
1	6	7	9	8	3	4	5	2
2	5	9	6	7	4	3	8	1
8	3	4	5	2	1	6	9	7
9	2	5	3	1	6	8	7	4
6	4	8	7	9	2	1	3	5
7	1	3	8	4	5	9	2	6

Page **87**

Page 88

Answer: C.
The inner shapes swap with the outer shape. The outer shape's outline colour swaps with that of the central inner shape. The outer shape's colour swaps with that of the other inner shapes

Page 89

Answer: 48% percent is blue, 52% is orange. 12 out of 25 triangles that make up the shape are blue, 13 are orange.

Multiply both numbers by 4 and you see a percentage

Page 90

Solution: 17

Page 91

Page 92

Answer: A pink face with a smile. Two different expressions (smile or frown) are followed by a pink face. Two faces the same colour are followed by a smile

Page 93

F	B	A	E	C	D
D	F	C	A	B	E
C	A	E	D	F	B
B	E	F	C	D	A
A	C	D	B	E	F
E	D	B	F	A	C

Answers

Page 94
Answer: Stonehenge

Page 95

Solution: Each vertical and horizontal line contains a picture with one star, a picture with two stars, and a picture with no stars.

Each line contains two full moons and a quarter moon. Each line contains a picture where the far right–hand building has three lights, a picture where it has two lights and a picture where it has one light.

The last picture must have two stars and a quarter moon, and the far right–hand building must have three lights

Page 96
Answer: D

Page 97

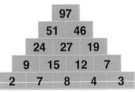

Page 98

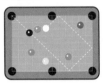

Page 99
Answer: B

Page 100
Answer: Bobby. There are 290 sweets in the jar

Page 101

9	6	2	4	1	8	5	3	7
1	4	5	2	3	7	9	6	8
3	8	7	5	9	6	1	2	4
6	7	1	9	8	2	3	4	5
4	3	8	1	6	5	2	7	9
5	2	9	3	7	4	8	1	6
2	1	4	6	5	9	7	8	3
7	9	3	8	4	1	6	5	2
8	5	6	7	2	3	4	9	1

Answers

Page 102
Solution: 22

 3

4

5

10

Page 103
Answer: 50.
22 red, 11 yellow and
17 orange

Page 104
Answer:
Blue = 1, Yellow = 2, Red = 3,
Purple = 4, Green = 5.
Three red balls are required

Page 105
Answer: Cream

Page 106
Answer:

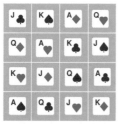

Page 107

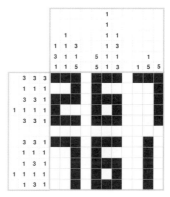

Page 108

Page 109
Answer: A and F are the pair

Answers

Page 110
Answer: Add the top two red corners, then add the bottom two. Then multiply the two totals.

$3 + 1 = 4$.
$8 + 2 = 10$.
$4 \times 10 = 40$.

Page 111
Answers:
A) 24 - multiply the opposite numbers.
B) 5 - divide the opposite numbers.

Page 112

Page 113
Answer: 28 revolutions of cog A, which will make exactly 35 revolutions of cog B and 20 revolutions of cog C.

Page 114
Answer: £100

Page 115
Solution: If its bordering squares (not diagonals) are predominantly pink, a square becomes blue.

If they are predominantly blue it becomes pink. If the bordering squares are equal in number, the square becomes yellow, and if the bordering squares have now become predominantly yellow, it also becomes yellow.

Page 116
Answer: A and I are the pair.

Page 117
Solution: If its bordering cells are predominantly green, a cell becomes grey. If they are predominantly grey, it becomes green. If the bordering cells are equal in number, the colour of a cell changes

Answers

Page 118
Answer: Up

Page 119
Answer: C

Page 120

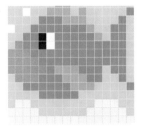

Page 121

Page 122

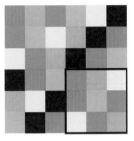

Page 123
Answer: Stick the signpost back up. If the sign to Aystown is pointing the way they have just come, then the rest of the signs will be pointing the right way.

Page 124
Answer: L1, E2, M16, C13

Page 125

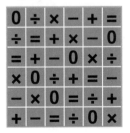

Answers

Page 126

5	1	6	7	2	3	4	9	8
4	3	9	1	8	6	2	7	5
2	8	7	9	5	4	6	1	3
6	7	3	2	1	9	5	8	4
1	4	5	6	7	8	9	3	2
9	2	8	3	4	5	1	6	7
3	5	1	8	6	2	7	4	9
7	9	2	4	3	1	8	5	6
8	6	4	5	9	7	3	2	1

Page 127
Answer: 49

Page 128

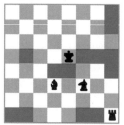

Page 129

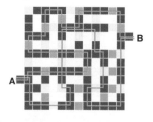

Page 130
Answer: 1

Page 131
Answer: D is the odd one out

Page 132

Page 133

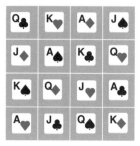

Answers

Page 134
Answer: F

Page 135
Answer:
purple 1
pink 2
green 3
red 4

Page 136
Answer: P11, B13, M14, H2

Page 137
Answer: 3650 square
millimetres.
Each 20 × 20 square
represents 400 mm².
4 squares, 6 half–squares,
2 half–square triangles,
3 quarter–squares and
3 8th of a square triangles
are used

Page 138

2	5	1	6	4	3
4	6	3	2	1	5
6	3	5	4	2	1
3	4	6	1	5	2
1	2	4	5	3	6
5	1	2	3	6	4

Page 139

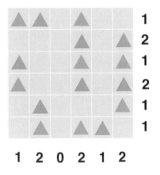

1
2
1
2
1
1

1 2 0 2 1 2

Page 140

Page 141

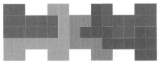

173

Answers

Page 142

Answer: A. Each row and column in the grid contains three stars, two targets with a red outer ring and one with a blue outer ring

Page 143

3	2	2	2	3
3	1	1	2	2
3	0	2	2	2
3	2	3	2	3
3	1	2	2	2

Page 144

23	18	19
16	20	24
21	22	17

Page 145

Answer: 720

The numbers represent the number of sides in the shape they occupy. When shapes overlap, the numbers are multiplied

3 x 3 x 4 x 4 x 5 = 720

Page 146

Answer:
3.25 am on Thursday in Karachi.
5.25 pm on Wednesday in Rio

Page 147

Answer: A

Page 148

Answer: 16

Multiply the alphabetical position of the first letter of each name by the number of vowels it contains. H = 8 and Hong Kong contains 2 vowels. 8 x 2 = 16

Page 149

Solution: Each horizontal and vertical line contains a red, a blue and a green neckerchief.

Each line contains one one–eared bear. Each line contains a full mouth, a left half–mouth and a right half–mouth. Each line contains two sticking plasters, one left and one right.

The missing picture should have a red neckerchief, have two ears, a right half–mouth and a sticking plaster on the left

Answers

Page 150
Answer: H

Page 151

0	2		5		5		5		5		2
		4			8		8		8		5
2			7	8		6		5		5		2
	5		8				6		6		3	
4		8		7	6		5		4		1
	7		7		5				7		5
3		5		4		3	5		8		4
	6		4		0		3				8
3		5		4		3		6	8		5
	7		7		5		6		8		
3		6		8		8		7		4	3
	2		4		5		5		4		1

Page 152

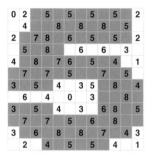

Page 153

Page 154

4	1	5	8	3	6	7	2	9
9	2	8	1	4	7	3	6	5
3	6	7	2	9	5	1	4	8
2	5	9	3	7	1	4	8	6
8	3	6	4	2	9	5	1	7
1	7	4	6	5	8	2	9	3
5	8	3	9	1	2	6	7	4
6	4	2	7	8	3	9	5	1
7	9	1	5	6	4	8	3	2

Page 155

Your puzzle notes